monday

The WORLD'S BEST OPTICAL ILLUSIONS

The WORLD'S BEST OPTICAL ILLUSIONS

Charles H. Paraquin

HARCOURT BRACE & COMPANY

Orlando Atlanta Austin Boston San Francisco Chicago Dallas New York
Toronto London

Translated by Paul Kuttner

Grateful acknowledgment is made to
Sterling Publishing Co., Inc., 387 Park
Avenue South, New York, NY 10016, for
permission to reprint *The World's Best
Optical Illusions* by Charles H. Paraquin,
translated by Paul Kuttner. Originally
published in hardcover under the title *Eye
Teasers*. © 1977 by Sterling Publishing Co.,
Inc. Original edition published in West
Germany under the title *Schummelbilder*.
© 1975 by Otto Maier Verlag Ravensburg.

Printed in the United States of America

ISBN 0-15-302230-2

4 5 6 7 8 9 10   011   97 96 95 94

Optical illusions are pictures that play tricks on your eyes and baffle your perception. They are not the result of faulty vision or psychic suggestion. Depending on light, viewing angle, or the way the picture is drawn, we may see things that aren't there—and often don't see what's right under our nose. Why does it happen?

Sometimes the answer lies in the way our eyes work. When we use both eyes, we see an object from two slightly set-apart angles. Each one registers a different view. If we use only one eye, look what happens:

1

Close your left eye. Keep your right eye focussed on the dog and move the book back and forth in front of you. At one point, the cat disappears completely. You have just found your blind spot. Everyone has one. It is the spot where the optic nerve cord leaves your eye, and there are no nerve cells to register an image. If you use both eyes as you look at the dog, you won't have a blind spot. The image from your left eye will make up for the blank in your right.

5

The shortcomings of our vision explain some types of optical illusions, but not all of them. Our eyes gather impressions, but it is the brain that interprets them. And the brain is always trying to make sense out of what it sees. So in spite of the fact that we know how perspective works, we go to the theatre or the movies and imagine that we're in a different world, tricked by a stage set and special effects. We watch magic acts and believe what reflecting mirrors show us. Illusion is everywhere—in art and architecture, in fashion and advertising, in the street and on television, even in the supermarket. If our eyes see something that the brain can't figure out, our minds "correct" the picture automatically.

Here is another illusion:

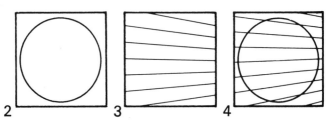

The box in the first picture contains an ordinary circle. The second box contains a field of slanted lines. Put them together and look what happens. The circle appears to become an oval and the box seems to be completely lop-sided. Test them with a ruler and compass. You'll see that they are exactly the same as they were before.

The human eye isn't as perfect as a camera lens, but that doesn't mean it is defective—just the opposite. Its adaptability is its strongpoint. In the semi-dark, for instance, our eyes function amazingly well. After about half an hour, our vision completely adjusts to the dark and its sensitivity increases 50,000 times! In the dark, we can see a burning candle from nearly 20 miles (32 kilometers) away!

Birds of prey (eagles and hawks) have much better vision than humans do in daylight. They see farther, but they suffer from night-blindness. Some other animals (owls, hedgehogs, cats) see well at night, but do not have very keen eyesight. So as human beings, we are lucky. We can see reasonably well during both day and night.

Humans are not the only ones who are tricked by optical illusions, either. Laboratory tests performed on fish and birds lead to the startling conclusion that these animals are fooled just about as often as we are, and sometimes in the same way!

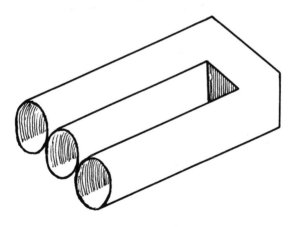

5 Deception? Illusion? Or just a careless artist?

Scientists have studied optical illusions for centuries, but they still don't agree about how or why all of them work. You'll see many different types of illusions in this book—geometric tricks, physiological tricks and psychological illusions—and you'll learn how many of them operate. But by no means are these *all* the optical illusions that are possible. The number of tricks you can play on your eyes is almost inexhaustible. These illusions are simply meant to amuse you, inspire you to explore this delightful scientific hobby yourself and perhaps even invent some new illusions of your own.

One suggestion: as you turn to each picture, look at it first with your naked eye. Don't check it out with a ruler or tracing paper until afterwards—when you can't believe your eyes!

6 A practical-looking construction. Can you build it?

7 Twin brothers: one of them has a bigger appetite. Which one?

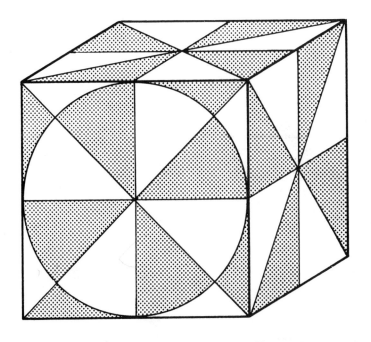

8 Is this cube higher and wider in the back than
in the front?

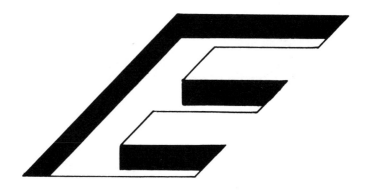

9 Is this letter "E" toppling forward or sinking down? Look at it steadily for half a minute.

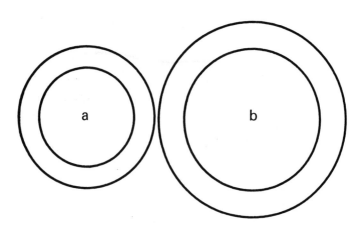

10 Is the outside circle of "a" smaller than the inside circle of "b"?

11 Which of these movie-goers is the tallest?

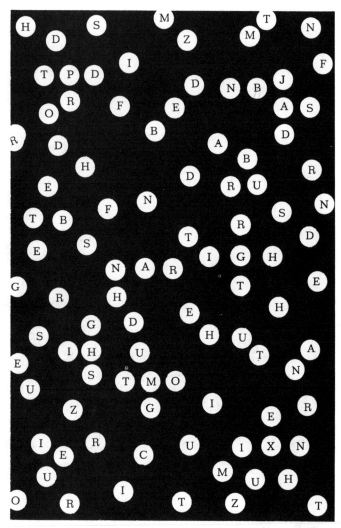

12 In this crowd of dots, there are five in the shape of a cross. Can you pick them out?

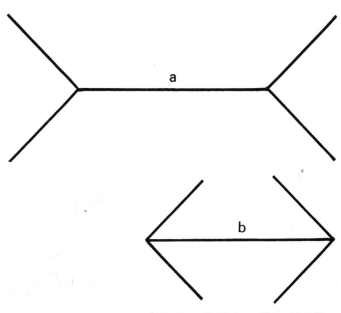

13 How much longer is line "a" than line "b"?

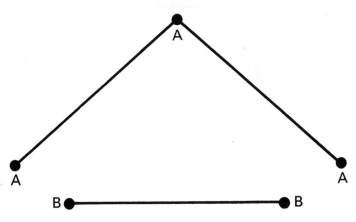

14 Are the two sides labeled "AA" each the same size as "BB"?

The ancient Greeks cheated.

That beautiful temple architecture, which seems so flawless and symmetrical, looks that way only with the help of some shrewd tricks.

The Greeks made the roof and the base (the horizontal lines) look straight by curving them upwards in the middle with edges turned towards the ground. If they had actually left the horizontal lines straight, the line would seem to sag in the middle.

The architects tampered with the columns (the vertical lines), too. Because vertical lines seem thinner in the middle than at the ends, they built the columns with a little bulge in the center.

That's not all. The columns also lean together at the top—just a few degrees; otherwise they would seem to spread out as they went up.

If you take the trouble to measure the temples' colonnades and arcades, you'll see that the distance between the columns varies. This was no accident. Bright colors, placed in front of darker ones, seem wider than they do against a light background. Therefore, the columns in front of the shadowy areas would seem much wider. The architects took this into account. The ancient Greeks knew all about optical illusions and used them to give the *illusion* of symmetry and perfection.

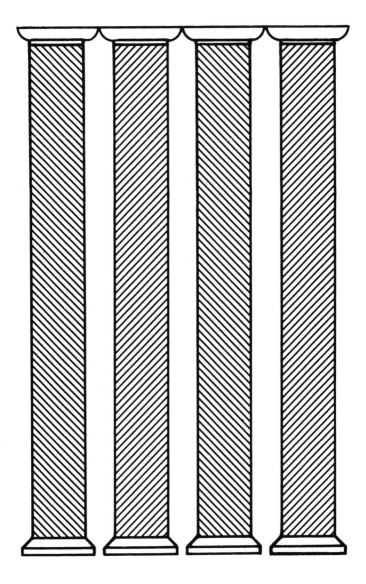

15 What is the matter with these columns?

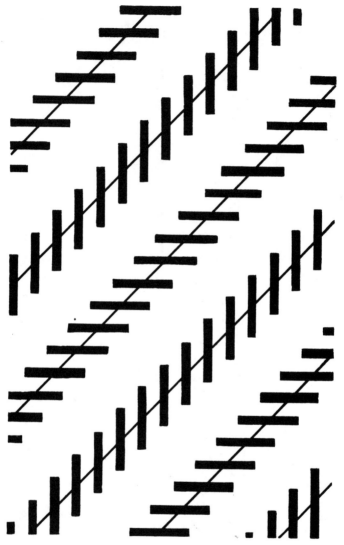

16 Are the thin lines parallel to each other? Or crooked?

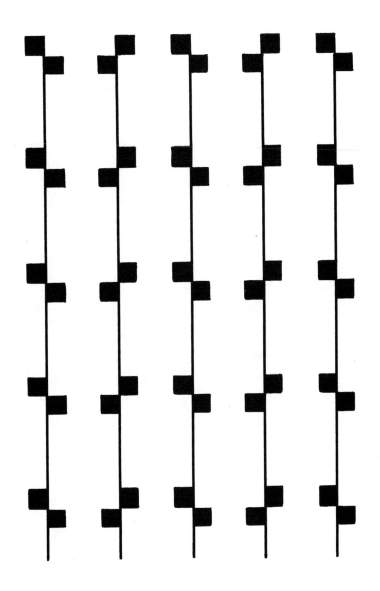

17 Are the vertical lines straight?

It depends on how you look at it.

These drawings seem to change, depending on where you place your attention. Because of the way the artist drew them, or the way the light seems to hit them, you can see them in two different ways. But you can only see one picture at a time! Which way is right? Both ways are. When people look at them, they see what they expect to see, what their experience tells them is most likely. Different people could see them either way, to start with. Take a look . . . take two looks.

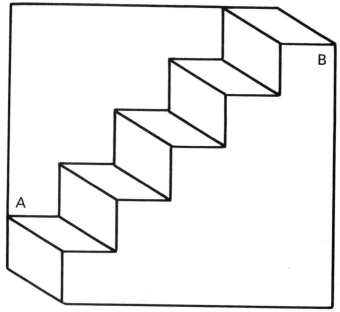

18 A normal staircase? Try walking on it upside down!

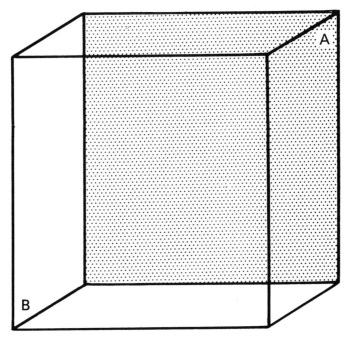

19 Which side of this cube is in front and which is in back? Look at it steadily.

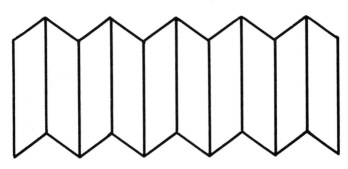

20 Are these 5 rooftops of connected houses? Or is this a 10-part folding screen?

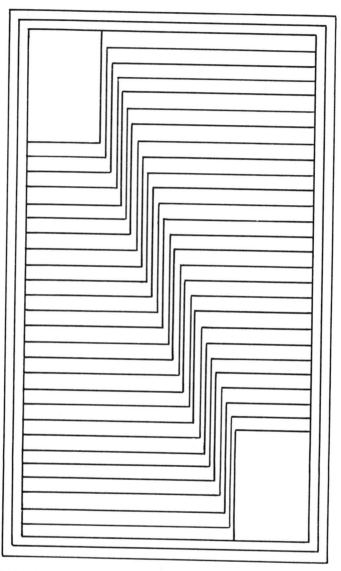

21 Is the left side of this picture high or the right side?

22

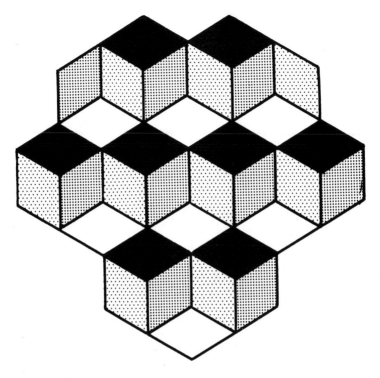

22 Are there 7 cubes here? Or 8 ?

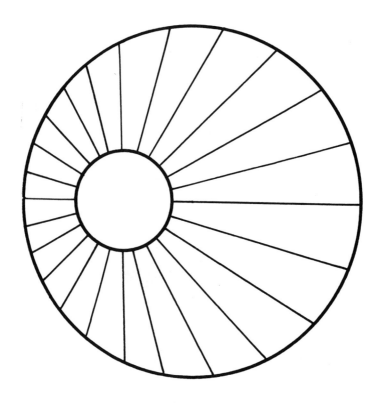

23 Are you looking inside a tube? Or at the top
of a beach ball?

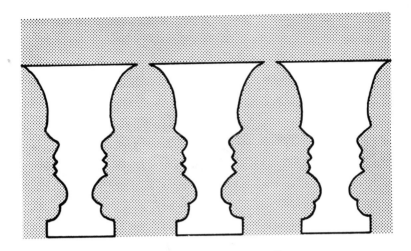

24 Faces—or vases?

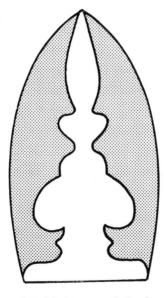

25 Light—or fight?

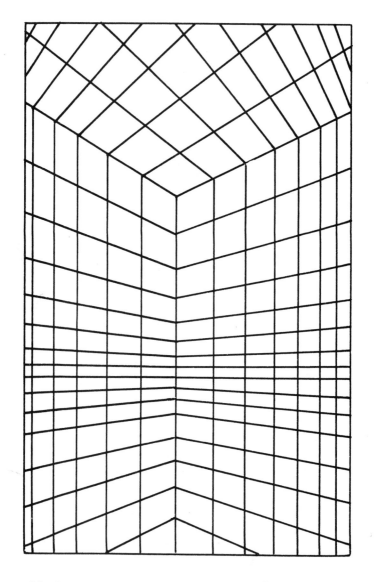

26 A strange room: are we inside it—or outside?

27 Which detective has the largest mouth?

Sometimes you can't see what's there . . .

Look at the shapes at the bottom of this page. If anyone told you that you wouldn't be able to find them—even though you were looking right at them—would you believe it?

The drawings that follow show how difficult it can be to see familiar shapes and figures when they are in unfamiliar surroundings. Each shape is hidden *once* (same size) in its corresponding diagram. For example, shape number 28 is hidden in drawing 28. Can you find it with your naked eye? Try this without using tracing paper and pencil—at first!

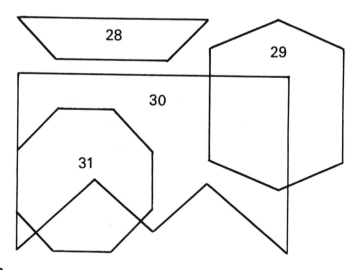

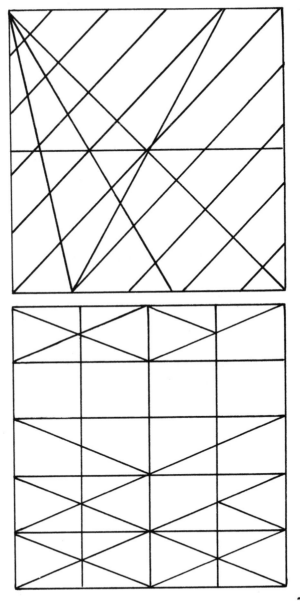

28

29

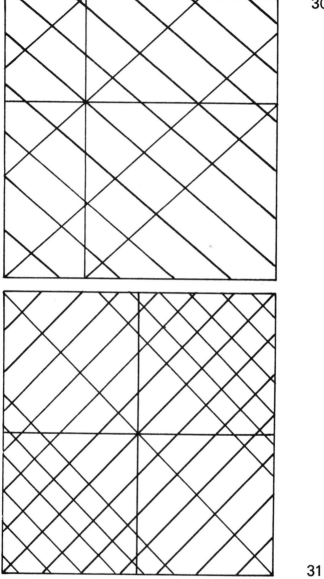

32

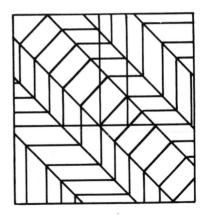

shape

32

shape

33

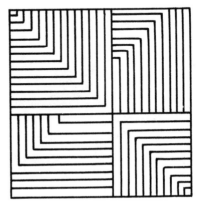

33

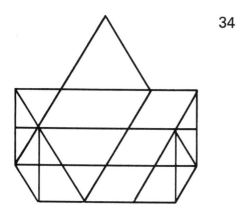

34

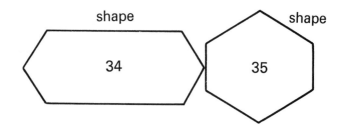

shape

shape

34

35

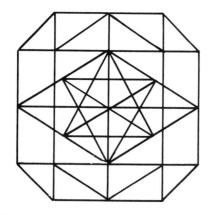

35

32

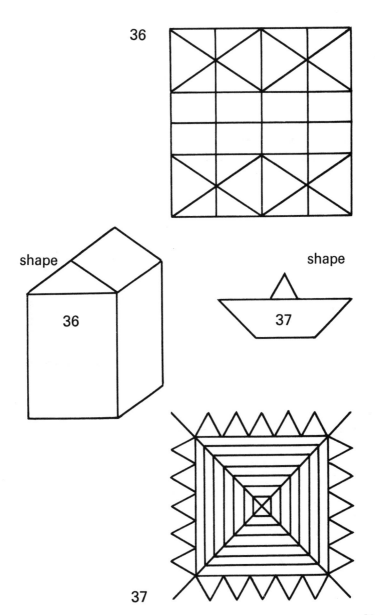

36

shape

36

shape

37

37

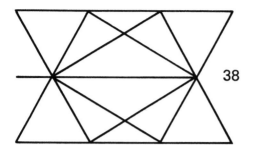

38

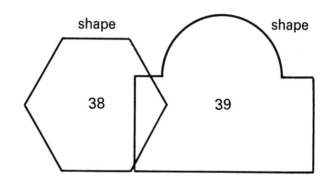

shape

shape

38

39

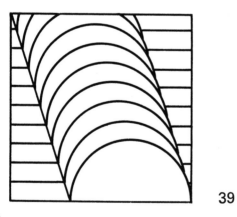

39

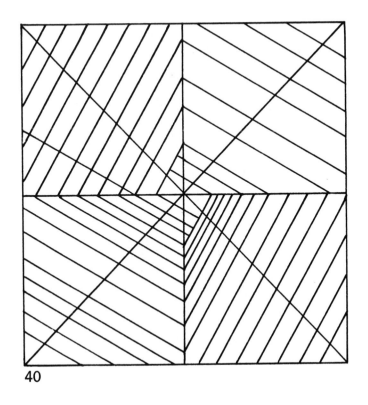

40

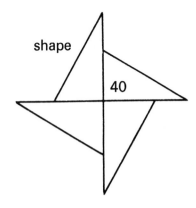

shape

40

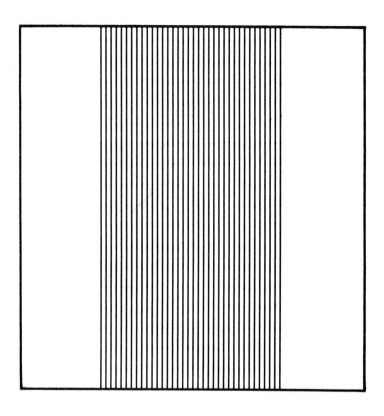

41 One window has vertical slats. The other has Venetian blinds. Which window is higher

and which is wider?

42 Is the rectangle an exact square—or are its sides collapsing?

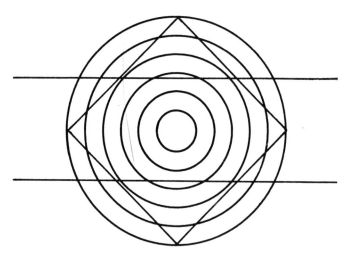

43 Are the horizontal lines parallel to each other?

44 What is happening to the diamond shape?

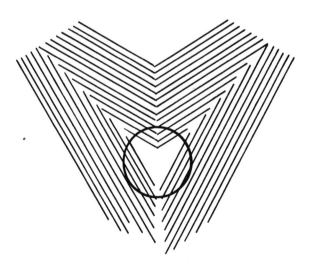

45 What is the matter with this circle?

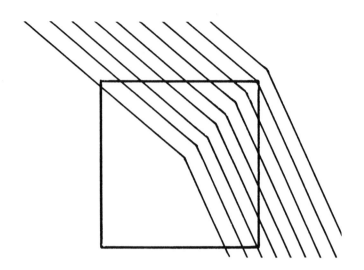

46 Is this a perfect square?

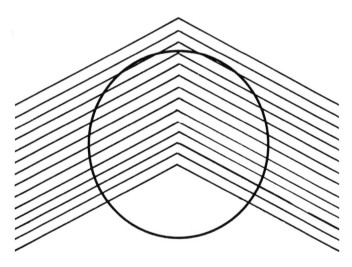

47 Isn't this circle flat at the top?

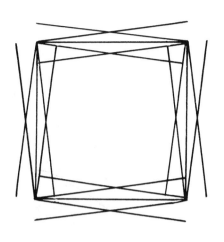

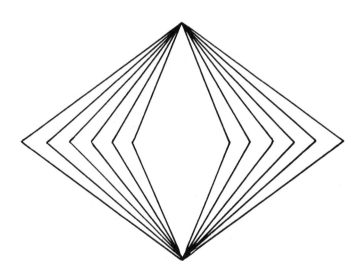

48 & 49 How many squares are there in these drawings?

50 Are the sides of this square bulging out?

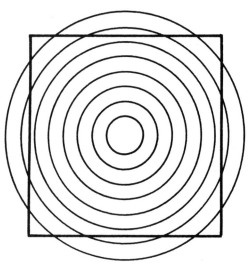

51 Are the sides of this one caving in?

52 Holding the page flat in front of you, move the book in a circle clockwise. What happens to the outside circles? What happens to the cogwheel in the middle?

Sometimes you see what isn't there at all . . .

Seeing isn't everything. After the light impressions are gathered and sent to the brain, our minds try to put them together into something understandable. We want it to make sense, to be familiar, to be safe, so we can go on about our business. We do this automatically—even if parts of a picture are not connected—even if parts of it are missing!—until we perceive a harmonious, satisfying "whole" that makes sense to us.

Once we find a familiar pattern, it's difficult to break up the idea, to separate its parts. The new form can become an optical illusion. We can't concentrate on just part of it, because our imaginations keep putting back what we try to block out of our minds!

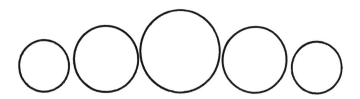

53 Do these circles sit on level ground, or do they arch upwards?

54 If parts of this picture are missing, our imaginations draw them in.

55 Moon tricks: which moon seems larger, the

one at the horizon or the one high in the sky?

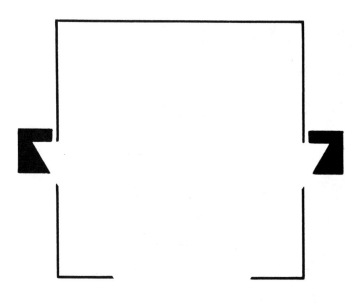

56 What white shape seems to be placed in front of the square?

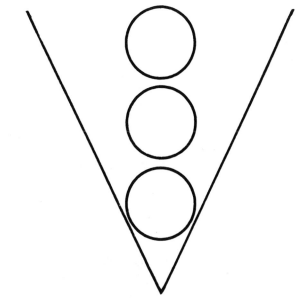

57 Which circle is the largest?

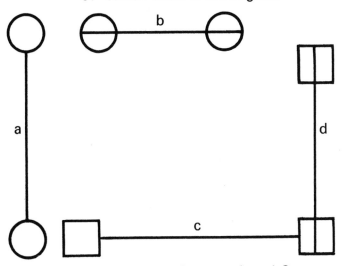

58 Which lines are the same length?

59 Which Easter egg fits into which egg cup?

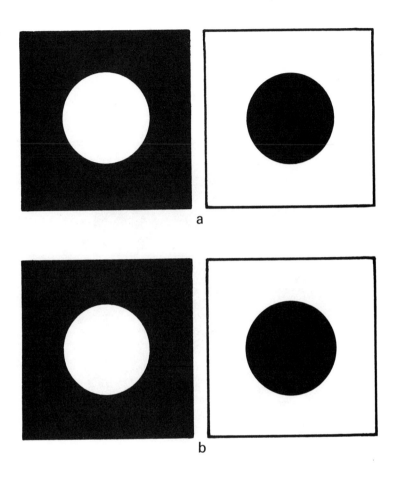

a

b

60 Which of the circles are the same size?
Those in row "a" or those in row "b"?

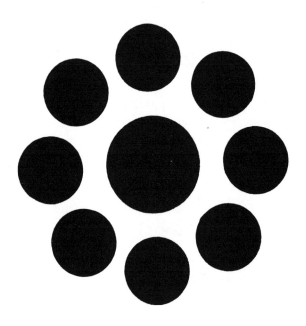

61 Which inner circle is larger—the one on the left?

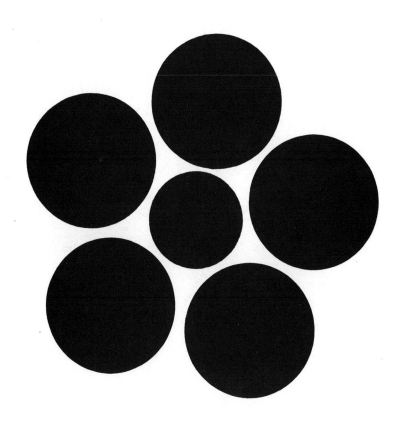

Or the one on the right?

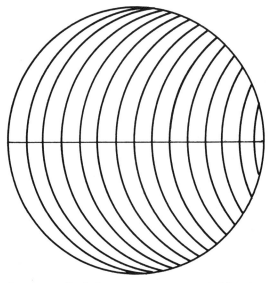

62 Can you find the exact center of this circle?

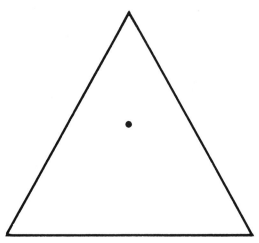

63 Is the dot midway between the point and the base of this triangle? Or is it too high up?

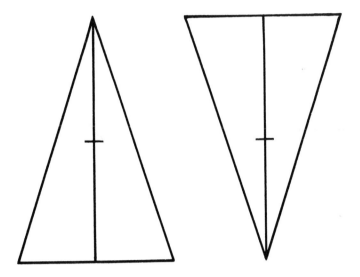

64 Are the cross-bars exactly in the middle of the center line of these triangles?

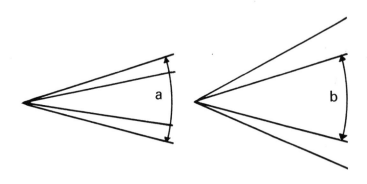

65 Is "a" larger than "b"?

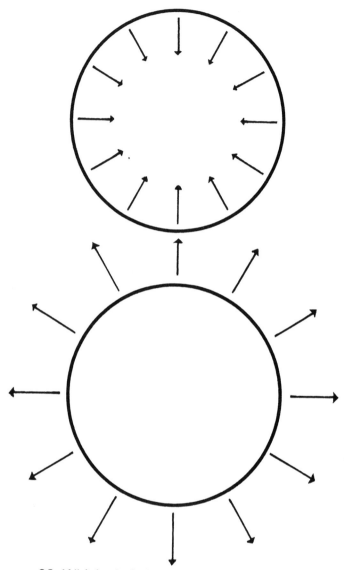

66 Which circle has the greater diameter?

67 Which is the longest object in this picture?

68 Which grey area is brighter?

Back and forth — up and down

Some scientists say it is "easier" to figure the distance between two points which lie on a horizontal level than those on vertical lines. We can guess the distance from house to house, for example, or tree to tree—far more accurately than the distance between a house and a plane which just appeared on the horizon. Others say we've had more experience with horizontal distances, and there is less we have to take into account. Usually we overestimate vertical distances, even if they are just down on the paper in front of us. Try your eye on some ups and downs.

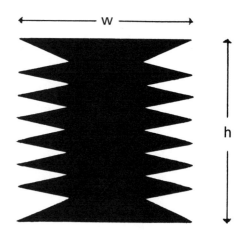

69 How does height ("h") correspond in size with width ("w") ?

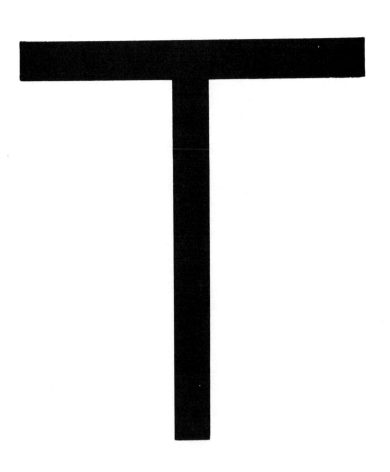

70 Which is longer—the vertical or the horizontal part of the "T" ?

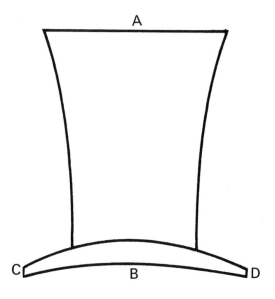

71 How does the height of this top hat ("A-B")
   compare with the width of its brim ("C-D")?

72 Is this top hat taller than its brim?

73 Is the church tower longer than the base of the church?

After-images

After you concentrate on a picture for a while, your eyes get tired. The most tired parts are certain spots on the "retina," the part of the eye which contains light-sensitive cells. The brightest tones cause the greatest stress to these cells, which gradually become less sensitive to light. When you look away from the picture and focus on a sheet of blank white paper, the nerve-ends which are *less* tired will lightly reproduce the darker sections of the picture. Your eye transforms a negative into a positive!

74 What shows up on the intersecting white lines, even though they are all white?

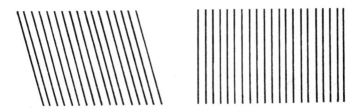

75 Concentrate for a while on the slanting lines.
Then shift to the vertical lines. What do you
see?

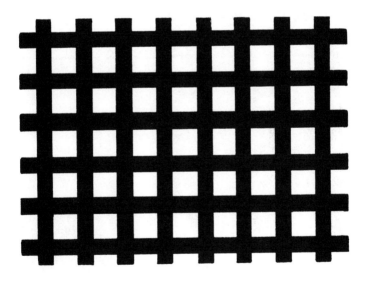

76 What do you see when you focus on the
black lines where they cross each other?

77 Focus hard on this negative for 30 seconds.
Then quickly switch your eyes to the blank

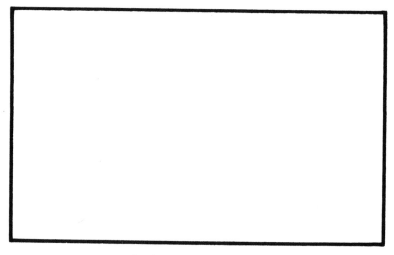

space at the bottom. What do you see?

78 Concentrate very hard on a point in the white
field of intersecting lines for about 30 seconds. Then shift your attention quickly to
one of the black squares. What do you see
inside the black squares?

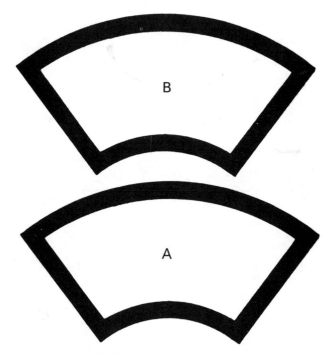

79 Are "A" and "B" the same size?

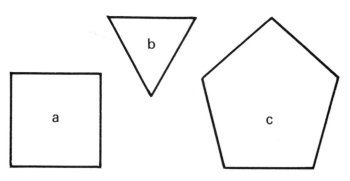

80 Which figure has the longest sides?

81 The spoke-wheel phenomenon: If you rotate
this, or look steadily at it, what do you see?

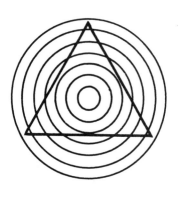

82 & 83 What is the matter with these triangles?

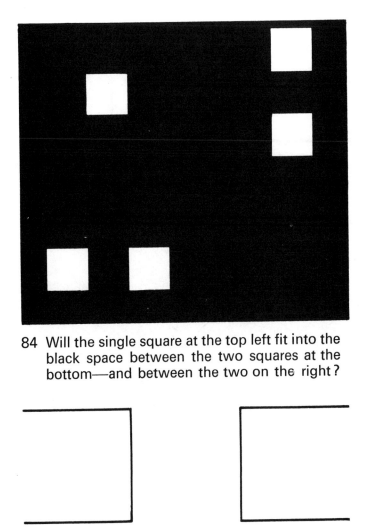

84 Will the single square at the top left fit into the black space between the two squares at the bottom—and between the two on the right?

85 Here are three incomplete squares. You can see three sides of the ones at the left and the right, but only two sides of the one in the middle. Which square is the smallest?

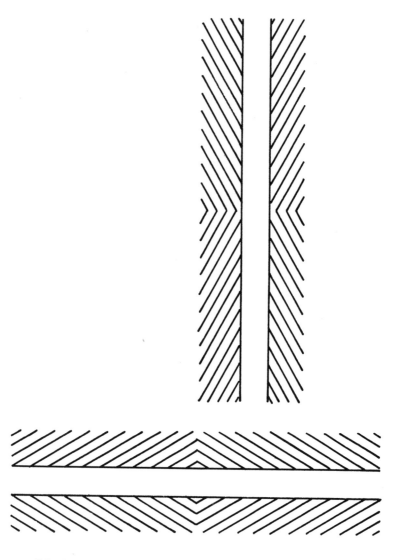

86 Are the white bars straight or do they bulge and bend?

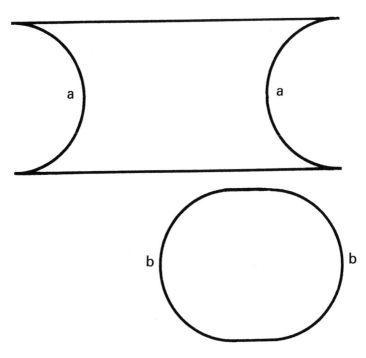

87 Is "a-a" the same length as "b-b"?

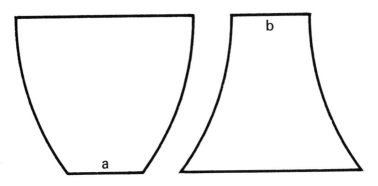

88 Which glass has a wider base?

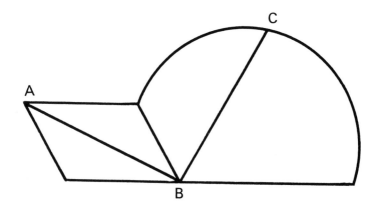

89 Which line is longer—"AB" or "BC"?

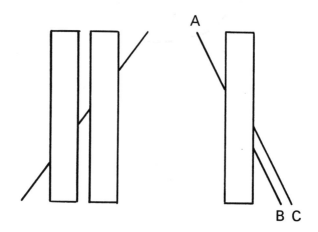

90 Is the diagonal line straight?

91 Which line is the continuation of "A"—"B" or "C"?

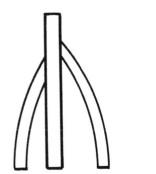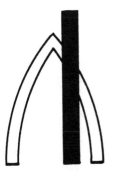

92 Are these pointed arches continuous or broken?

93 Are the vertical lines straight? Do the cross-bars go straight through them or is their pattern uneven?

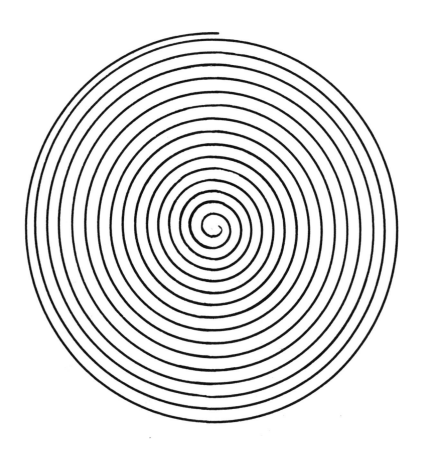

94 Turn this book in a circle clockwise. Then
turn it in a circle counter-clockwise. Is there
a difference, besides just their direction?

95 A star is hidden among all these designs. It is a 4-pointed star, about $1\frac{1}{2}$ inches (4 cm.) long from tip to tip. Can you find it?

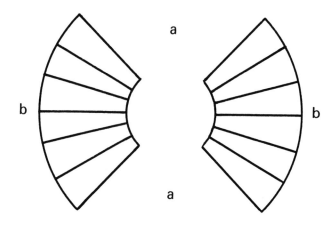

96 Are the lined-in sections ("b") of the circle larger than the open sections ("a") ?

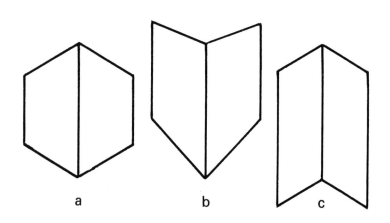

a b c

97 Is the center line ("a") shorter than

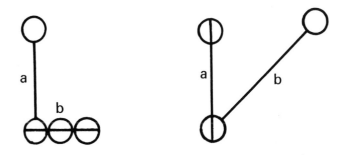

98 Which is longer, line "a" or line "b"?

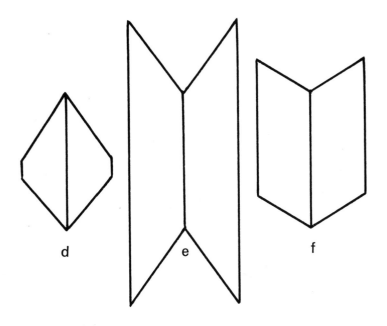

the others ("b" to "f")?

Little things mean a lot . . .

The first thing we see in any picture is usually the most obvious, most striking part. We often overlook smaller things, even though they may hold the key to a more important pattern.

If you concentrate on a design in some fabric or wallpaper, you see the simple pattern in the foreground first. You may think that because you've noticed the pattern, you have seen and understood the design. Usually you haven't.

Test yourself on this. Try to make a sketch from memory of what you remember of the design. Suddenly something is wrong. You can't complete the drawing because your mind simplified the design. It blocked out important parts of the picture.

The designs in the next diagrams have been put together from geometric forms. Can you tell which simple shape forms the basis for each pattern?

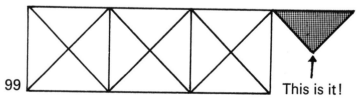

99

This is it!

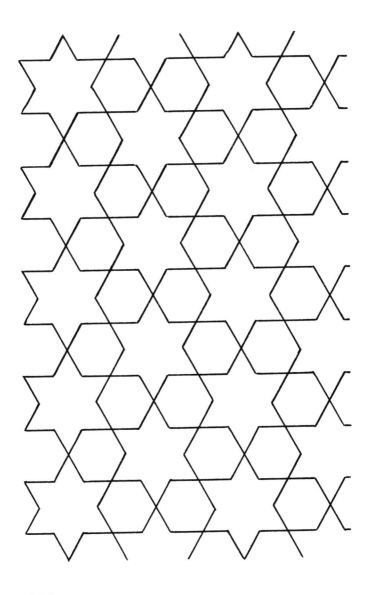

100

101

102

103

104

Find the hidden object . . .

You're looking at a drawing of a street scene. There are shops, people walking, children playing. But is there something else? You look a little closer and sure enough, certain parts of the drawing turn into birds—or foxes— or monsters!

These are "hidden object" pictures. You've probably seen them many times. The objects aren't really hidden; they're just camouflaged within other shapes. Once you discover them, they're as hard to ignore as they were to find.

These hidden object puzzles are optical illusions, too. They depend on a trick. The artist blended the outlines of the hidden objects with the outlines of other, more conspicuous shapes. Of course, we focus on the more obvious patterns in the foreground. In order to find the hidden objects, you may have to turn the picture left, right, upside down, or maybe you need to squint!

105 Where are the hidden fish in this meadow?

106 Can you find the owners of this house ?

107 What happened to the three boys who were
gathering mushrooms?

Answers 1-14

1 See page 5.
2, 3 & 4 See page 6.
5 Illusion. This is an impossible creation.
6 Never. This is a trick drawing.
7 There's no way to tell. The twin with the horizontal stripes seems to be fatter, but he really isn't. Our eyes follow the lines in his suit, so the twin on the right seems broader and shorter than his brother.
8 No, but it seems higher and wider in the back because of the way it has been drawn. We expect the back of it to be further away and to look smaller. Since it is the same size, we automatically assume it is bigger in the back.
9 Both are possible. It depends on how you look at it.
10 No, but it seems to be, because "b" is in a larger area.
11 They are all the same height. The man at the right looks tallest. We expect things to look smaller when they are farther away. The man at the right is farthest away and we would expect him to look the smallest. Since he doesn't, we assume he's really larger than the others.
12 The dot-shaped cross is just to the right of the center of the diagram. It spells out "R-I-G-H-T." It may take you a while to find it, because the other dots distract your attention.
13 They are the same length. Our eyes follow the lines. The "a" line seems to expand because of the "wings" on the ends. Line "b" is cut off by its arrowheads, so it looks shorter.
14 Exactly. They seem longer in relation to their surroundings.

Answers 15-31

15 Nothing, except that the stripes make them look as if they are rocking back and forth. They are exactly parallel to each other.

16 Exactly parallel. The thicker cross-hatch lines just give the illusion that they are bending. Some scientists say this is because we cannot judge the size of angles well. Others say the cross-lines distract us.

17 Yes, they run parallel to each other.

18 Depending on how you focus on the letters, the staircase can run up from A to B or you could be standing beneath the upside-down version. To see it upside down, focus on the A.

19 Either one, depending on where you place your attention. When you look at the "A," the dotted wall seems to be in front. When you look at the "B," it seems to be in back.

20 It could be either one.

21 Depending on the way you look at it, either side.

22 Both. There are 8 cubes with black tops or 7 cubes with white bottoms.

23 Either.

24 It depends whether you place your attention on the dark or light color. Either one can be the background.

25 Same.

26 Either one.

27 The four detectives have equally large mouths.

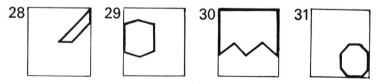

28   29   30   31

Answers 32-50

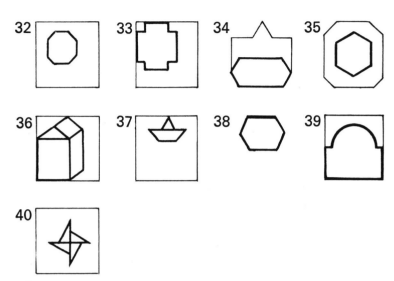

41 They are both the same height and width. The one with the horizontal stripes looks wider because your eyes follow the horizontal lines.

42 It is an exact square, but when it is broken by other lines, our eyes are distracted and follow the new lines instead of the original square.

43 Yes. The other lines distract from them and make them seem to bend a little, but they are parallel.

44 Nothing; it is a perfect square, but the distracting shape makes it seem warped.

45 Nothing. It is an exact circle.

46 Yes.

47 No, it is a perfect circle.

48 There is one exact square.

49 Same.

50 No. Our eyes cannot separate the figure from the intercepting arcs. Nevertheless, it is a perfect square.

Answers 51-62

51 No, but the circle makes it look that way.

52 The circles spin to the right. Many people say the cogwheel turns to the left; others say it stands still.

53 They all sit on level ground.

54 See page 45.

55 They are the same size. Scientists tell us—even though we know better—that we still see the sky as a kind of flattened dome, and nearer to us than the horizon! When any object is close to the horizon then, we assume it is farther away than when it is overhead. Therefore, while the moon is always the same size, we trick ourselves into thinking that it is larger when it is near the horizon.

56 A triangle with equal sides.

57 They are all the same size.

58 Line "a" equals "b" and "c" equals "d." Line "a" seems longer than "b" because we unconsciously add the circles on the end of line to its length. The same is true of line "c" with its open square.

59 Each egg fits into all the egg cups.

60 In "a"—both are the same size, but the white one seems larger. When bright light falls on the retina of our eyes (where the nerve cells are), more nerve fibres react than actually had the light hit them. This causes a "spreading effect," and the light object seems larger than it actually is. In "b," the black circle is actually larger, although both seem to be the same size.

61 The inner circles are the same size. The one on the right looks smaller because we usually judge the size of an object by contrasting it with the objects around it.

62 Measure it. The curved lines force our eyes to move to the left of the true center.

Answers 63-78

63 It is exactly in the center.

64 The cross-bars are exactly in the center of the triangles.

65 No, they are both the same size. This is another example of the difficulty of judging size when angles are involved.

66 Both circles are the same size. The arrows pull our eyes inwards in the top circle, and our eyes follow the arrows outwards in the lower one.

67 All the objects are the same length.

68 Both grey areas have the same intensity. The white lines, though, make the area on the left seem brighter.

69 Height and width are the same.

70 The lines are the same length, but the vertical one seems longer. Some scientists say that the horizontal line looks shorter simply because it has been broken into two parts.

71 They are the same.

72 Tricked you? It's $\frac{1}{4}$ inch (6.25 mm.) longer!

73 Height is the same as the width (with tower).

74 You see grey dots at the point where white meets white. The white lines look brightest when they contrast with the black areas. When white meets white, therefore, they are less bright—and the grey dots appear.

75 The vertical lines seem to lean to the right.

76 Grey dots, as in 74.

77 You see an outline in positive form of the negative that is on the top.

78 Inside the black squares you see an even blacker lattice design! This is the result of your eyes being tired of seeing the white lines. They record the black instead, when you look away.

Answers 79-92

79 "A" seems larger, but they are both the same size. Our tendency is to compare the base of "B" with the top arch of "A."

80 All the sides are the same length. The sides of "C" look longer because of the area they enclose.

81 As you turn or as your eyes tire, the overlapping images cause you to see "moire" (plane propeller) designs within the circles.

82 Nothing, but your eyes follow the intersecting lines, and that makes the sides look crooked.

83 Same.

84 Yes, the square fits perfectly into both spaces. The square seems larger than the black space, because of the "spreading effect" of light.

85 They are all the same size. The central one looks taller and narrower because it is made of vertical lines only.

86 They are perfectly straight.

87 Yes. "a" seems larger because it intersects a larger area.

88 The glasses are equally wide at the base, but "a" seems longer because the glass is wider.

89 "AB" and "BC" are the same length. "BC" seems longer because it intersects a larger area.

90 Yes, but when you break a straight line with a solid bar, the straight line seems displaced.

91 "B" is the continuation of "A." "C" looks as though it connects with "A" because the solid bar "displaces" the line.

92 Continuous. It is the solid bar in front of them that makes them look broken.

Answers 93-107

93 They are straight. Tilt the book all the way back and you'll have proof! The cross-bar lines look displaced, which adds to the confusion.

94 Clockwise, the distance between the lines seems to constrict. Counter-clockwise, the distances between the lines appear to expand.

95 The star is to the left in the middle of the picture.

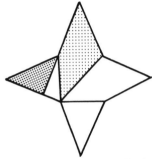

96 The quarters are all the same size.

97 The center-lines in drawings "a" to "f" are all the same height. The only differences are the angles of the lines leading away from them.

98 In each figure, "a" equals "b."

99 See page 80.

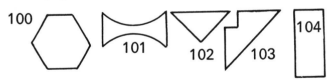

105 From the bottom to the top and left of the center.

106 There are two. One is on top, in the drapes; his wife is in the leaves of the potted palm.

107 They are in the trees.

Index